Walks Through R

Ten self-guided walks

by

Louise Allen

Fifth revised edition.

https://www.louiseallenregency.com/

Cover illustration: Leicester Square viewed from Leicester Place. (Ackermann's Repository of Useful Arts etc 1812)

Table of Contents

Introduction

Walk 1: St James 1-13

Walk 2: Hyde Park & Kensington Gardens 14-18

Walk 3: Mayfair North 19-25

Walk 4: Piccadilly & Mayfair South 26-34

Walk 5: Soho North 35-40

Walk 6: Soho South to Somerset House 41-48

Walk 7: The British Museum to Covent Garden 49-55

Walk 8: Trafalgar Square to Westminster Abbey 56-63

Walk 9: The City From Bridewell to the Bank 64-69

Walk 10: Southwark & the South Bank 70-74

About the Author 75

Introduction

This book is the result of many explorations in search of the Regency London that forms the background of my novels. London has a long history and fire, war and redevelopment have destroyed, changed and blurred the physical evidence of that past. Yet it can still be found, sometimes intact, sometimes only as a ghost.

These walks will take you to the London of the "long Regency" – the last years of the 18th century and into the first quarter of the 19th century. In some places you can see actual buildings and places that Jane Austen, Nelson or Beau Brummell would have recognised. In others the explorer must use their imagination to conjure up the past.

Following these trails will take you close to many of the other great sights of London from all periods. These have not been mentioned here in order to keep the focus on the late Georgian period, but a little planning with a standard guidebook will help the reader to adapt these walks to include those, if desired.

Each walk is around 2 miles (3 km) long, not allowing for visits inside museums, but they can be subdivided and tackled in shorter visits or linked together for all-day explorations.

Using this book.

This book has been designed so that you do not need a map. However, a tourist map app or a pocket map is helpful in locating tube stations and bus routes and in linking up walks. For hard copy I use *The Handy London Map and Guide* by Bensons MapGuides. Check relevant websites for any changes in hours etc before visiting.

Otherwise all you need are a comfortable pair of shoes and an active imagination!

Walk 1: St James's

Distance: 1.5 miles.

Transport: Nearest tube station – Green Park. Buses 9, 14, 19, 22, 23, 38.

When to visit: Spencer House is only open on Sundays (Guided tours. Booking required.) but St James's Square garden and the shops in St James's Street are closed then and services may be in progress in St James's church.

Useful websites:

St James's church: https://sjp.org.uk

Spencer House: https://spencerhouse.co.uk

Green Park: https://wwwroyalparks.org.uk/visit/parks/green-park

Start at Green Park tube, turn right along Piccadilly to St James's Street. Pause at the top of the street looking down to St James's Palace.

On the corner was the fashionable shoemaker George Hoby, who designed riding boots for the Duke of Wellington, resulting in the eponymous Wellington boot.

St James's Street was the masculine heart of fashionable Regency London. Georgette Heyer's fans will recall the scene in *The Grand Sophy* where Sophy disgraces herself by driving Miss Wraxton down St James's Street past the gentlemen's clubs.

In 1815 "the west side of this street is chiefly composed of stately houses belonging to the nobility and gentry, one or two extensive hotels, bankers etc. The opposite side consists of elegant shops, which appear to a stranger rather as lounging-places than resorts of trade and the busy pursuits of merchandise." But, as the Reverend Joseph Nightingale went on to point out: "The fact is, that, with one or two exceptions, these hotels are those sinks of vice and dissipation – the bane of human happiness and domestic peace – Gaming Houses!" (*Surveys of the City of London and the City of Westminster*, 4 vols 1814-15.)

It is estimated that there were twenty-four gaming hells in the St James's area at the beginning of the 19th century.

Also in St James's were the St James's Coffeehouse opposite the Palace gates, much frequented by army and navy officers; the Royal Coffeehouse where large parties met to dine; the Smyrna Coffeehouse, famous for billiards; the York and Dover coffee houses and Parsloe's subscription rooms with a chess club.

Walk down St James's Street on the right hand side.

You almost immediately come to the building that was Crockford's Club (no.50), opened in 1828. It was founded by William Crockford, an extraordinary figure who started as a fishmonger and became one of the wealthiest men in England. The club closed in 1970.

Stand here for a good view of White's opposite (nos.37-8), in a building dating from 1788. It originated in 1693 as a chocolate house and was not just the oldest, but also the smartest and most exclusive of the Regency clubs. It was home to the "Beau" Window set who would watch the world go by from their position of superiority seated in the bow window over the door. The door and window have now gone, but a Regency bow remains at ground level. On 16th May 1816 Beau Brummell fled England for ever as a result of a scandal that erupted at White's over a debt.

The street was not an entirely masculine preserve, however. In 1817 Mrs Bell moved to no.52. Her designs for gowns grace the pages of *La Belle Assemblée*, one of the premier fashion journals of the Regency.

Cross Bennett Street and pause in front of no.55.

In 1807 a Mrs Clark was advertising from her shop at no.56, "...a large assortment of corsets of every size, and superior make, so that ladies may immediately suit themselves without the inconvenience of being measured."

Boodles (no.28 opposite) is another old club, started in 1752 in Pall Mall and moving here in 1783. The premises were originally occupied by the Savoir Vivre, a notorious gaming hell. Boodles was a favourite of country squires and the hunting set.

Continue down St James's Street.

Brooks's club (no.60), on the northern corner of Park Place, was famous for high-stakes gambling and moved here from Pall Mall in 1778. Byron was a member. The interior today is hardly changed since his time.

Cross Park Place.

On the southern corner at no.61 is Justerini & Brooks, wine merchants (est.1749). At 63 was Fenton's Hotel, a favourite for gentlemen up from the country. It opened in 1800, was rebuilt in 1823 and demolished in 1887. Amongst its facilities were medicinal baths.

Continue downhill, turn right into the narrow entrance to Blue Ball Yard and walk along to the end.

Here you can see a well-preserved mews with 1740's stables and rooms above.

Return to St James's Street and continue down on the right-hand side.

No.64 is the site of the Cocoa Tree coffee house, later a club patronised by Byron and, a little further along at no.71, another old business in a modern building – barbers Trufitt & Hill (est.1805).

St James's Street is so wide that it proved a safety hazard for gentlemen rather the worse for drink after a long session at their clubs. As a result it was given the first traffic islands in London so the clubmen could take refuge half way across.

Cross the road and walk down to no.7.

Lobb's the bootmakers is at no.7. It is a relative newcomer, established in 1866. If it is open, go in to see the workshop where individual wooden lasts are still hand-made Display cases hold interesting historic footwear. Next door at no.8 is the site of Byron's apartments – imagine the furore Lady Caroline Lamb caused when she arrived here in boy's clothing to visit him. The visit was unwelcome and embarrassing and a friend had to persuade her to leave.

At no.6 are Lock & Co., the hatters, founded in the 17th century. The building is late 17th century with an 18th century brick frontage. They are tolerant of visitors wanting to look around. Inside, on shelves behind the lovely shop front (c.1810), you can see military headgear and early beaver top hats. The showcase at the foot of the stairs contains fascinating historical items, including a replica of the hat with a green eyeshade designed by them to Lord Nelson's specifications, and a hat that belonged to the Duke of Wellington.

Turn left out of Lock's and left again into the narrow entrance to Pickering Place.

In the passage note the old shutters from Berry Bros. & Rudd on the left-hand wall. Tiny Pickering Place is reputed to be the location in the 1840s of the last duel in London and was the home of the Texas Legation before Texas joined the USA. For Heyer fans it is mentioned in several books as the location of a gaming hell.

Retrace your steps to St James's Street, turn left to Berry Bros. & Rudd.

The beautiful early 19th century shopfront of Berry Bros. & Rudd hides an atmospheric interior with sloping wooden floors, panelling and the famous scales. If they are open, enter to see where Byron, the Prince Regent, William Pitt, Nelson and Lady Hamilton were all weighed. Their weights were recorded in books that are still kept up, although these days only members of the family are allowed on the antique balance. The business was founded here in 1698 as a grocer and coffee seller, as the hanging sign of a coffee grinder outside reveals, and moved into wine in the 18th century. There are vast cellars stretching under St James's.

Turn left out of Berry Bros. & Rudd.

On the other side of the street at no.80 was the home of Sir Francis Burdett, radical politician, supporter of Catholic emancipation and husband of the banking heiress Sophia Coutts.

At the end of St James's Street is St James's Palace, one of the chief royal residences until Buckingham House was enlarged for George IV in the 1830s. Four of his brothers resided here although, before his accession, the Prince Regent himself preferred Carlton House. Foreign ambassadors are still accredited to the Court of St James, although the monarch no longer lives there.

The largely Tudor building is not open to the public, except for the Queen's Chapel where the public may attend services on Sundays 8.30am and 11.30am, October to Good Friday.

The Palace's external appearance has changed very little and it is easy to conjure up the picture on the occasion of King George III's birthday on

June 4th. A grand Drawing Room was held each year and a birthday ode performed. In the evening the tradesmen holding royal warrants illuminated their shops and at five in the afternoon the Mail coaches formed a procession from the Post Office near St Paul's Cathedral to St James's and back.

Turn left into Pall Mall and walk towards Waterloo Place.

Pall Mall was laid out in 1661 on the site of the grassed *palle-maille* (pell-mall) alley. The game, somewhat similar to croquet, was very popular in the 17th century. The area soon filled up with courtiers' lodgings, clubs and taverns, including the original Almack's gaming house which was at no.50.

The street was lined with clubs, hotels, insurance agents and upmarket shops such as the fashionable drapers, Harding, Howell & Co. who had an early type of department store in Schomberg House. You come to this distinctive 17th century building with its dark red brick and white stonework on the right-hand side of the road. It was split into smaller units in the 18th century and has now been restored as one (nos. 80-82).

The quack doctor James Graham opened his "Temple of Health" here in the 1780s with the infamous Celestial Bed, stuffed with wild oats and hair from the tails of, naturally, stallions. Draperies, lights, mirrors, organ music and perfume and the enticements of "Vestina, Goddess of Health" created an exotic sensual playground.

Graham claimed that the bed, surrounded by lodestones or magnets, was an aid to pleasurable sex and the creation of healthy offspring. Charges to use it are said to have ranged from 50 guineas to £100 a night. (Over £8,000 in today's money).

In 1807 Pall Mall was the first London street to be gas-lit as a temporary display for the King's birthday, probably because of the influence of the

Gas Light and Coke Company whose office was on the south side. Its site is now marked by a plaque.

The area was a focus for art exhibitions during the Regency period, both by individual artists and in galleries, and Jane Austen records viewing an exhibition by Sir Joshua Reynolds here. The largest venue, the Gallery of the British Institution, was established by the King to encourage British art.

Pass the Reform Club (founded 1836, now in an 1841 building) at no.104 and you are where Carlton House was situated. Henry Holland had created this building of astounding opulence for the Prince Regent between 1783 and 1802. His daughter Princess Caroline was born there in 1796. She married Prince Leopold there in 1816 to huge popular rejoicing.

When the Prince Regent became George IV in 1820 he considered that Carlton House and St James's Palace were inadequate and had Buckingham House redeveloped as his main London residence. Carlton House was demolished in 1827.

Waterloo Place is the southern termination of John Nash's great Regent Street project and the location of the earliest work on the scheme. Swathes of houses were demolished and streets disappeared during 1816 and Waterloo Place was largely finished by 1818.

Various clubs were built here, along with some great mansions and Warren's Hotel. Considerable rebuilding occurred during the 19th century, as in all of Regent's Street, and, although the space gives a very good impression of Nash's original, every building you see is a later replacement.

Turn right and walk down Waterloo Place towards the Duke of York Column.

At the kerbside outside the Athenaeum Club is a granite mounting block: "Erected by desire of the Duke of Wellington 1830". Presumably the aging duke required some help after convivial evenings at his club.

The column was erected in 1832 in memory of Frederick, Duke of York and Albany, second son of King George III. He was commander-in-chief of the British Army and carried out many reforms. He is also the Grand Old Duke of York of the nursery rhyme. Go past the column for a view over St James's Park towards Westminster Abbey.

Retrace your steps and turn left into Carlton House Terrace.

When Carlton House was demolished, part of the site and the gardens were redeveloped by Nash between 1827 and 1833 into Carlton House Terrace. At 6-9 is The Royal Society, founded in 1660 and at the forefront of scientific discovery right through the 18th and 19th centuries to the present day.

Turn right into Carlton Gardens, note a plaque to Prime Minister Palmerston at no.4, cross Pall Mall and continue straight ahead to St James's Square.

St James's Square was developed by the Earl of St Albans in the 17th century, and is one of the earliest examples of formal London street planning. It was substantially rebuilt in the 18th century.

The statue of King William III was erected in 1808 and the square was lit by gas in 1817 when improvements were made to enlarge the central garden and to plant it with shrubs. The work was supervised by Nash who also designed the wooden garden shelter (1822). When the garden is open you can gain access on the northern side.

The square was highly fashionable and desirable, although gradually commercial and institutional occupants moved in. The Union Club occupied no.21 (1807-1816) and Wedgwood's china showrooms were at no.8 on the corner of Duke of York Street (1797-1829). In 1813, in a letter to her sister Cassandra, Jane Austen records visiting here in order to help their brother Edward choose a dinner service. "I believe the pattern is a small Lozenge in purple, between Lines of narrow Gold – & is to have the Crest."

John Stockdale the publisher set up shop in the square in 1826 and proceeded to publish instalments of the *Memoirs* of the notorious courtesan Harriette Wilson. She tried to blackmail the Duke of Wellington into paying not to be included, but he famously told her to, "Publish and be damned!" Her remarks about him in the book did little for his reputation as a lover.

It was at no.16, that the Prince Regent received the news of the victory at Waterloo on June 21st 1815 whilst at a dinner party.

In 1820 Caroline, his estranged queen, took up temporary residence at no.17 (now rebuilt) during her "trial". This was a parliamentary investigation into accusations of adultery by which means George, by then George IV, hoped to secure a divorce which could only be granted by Act of Parliament. She would set out from here for Westminster amidst huge crowds and near-riotous scenes of public support: she was far more popular than her husband.

Next door, Byron's daughter, Ada, Countess Lovelace, the pioneer of early computing, lived at no.12 and no.10 was home to three Prime Ministers at various times – Pitt the Elder, the Earl of Derby and Gladstone. In the north western corner is the London Library (no.14), where Georgette Heyer did much of her Regency research.

There is a fine view down Charles Street to the Theatre Royal Haymarket, built in 1820.

Leave the square by Duke of York Street in the centre of the northern side.

On the left as you walk up Duke of York Street is the tiny *Red Lion* pub, opened in 1821, although the front has been refaced. The interior is a perfect example of a mid-Victorian pub with all its fittings.

Cross Jermyn Street and enter St James's church, designed by Sir Christopher Wren.

The church is full of memorials, including several to significant Regency figures. Sir Richard Croft was the *accoucheur* who was attending the heir to the throne, Princess Charlotte, when she died in childbirth in 1817. Her death led to a rush to marry amongst the Royal Dukes and consequently, to the birth of Princess, later Queen, Victoria. Accused of negligence, Croft shot himself in 1818.

Other memorials include that to Lieutenant-General Sir Colin Campbell (d.1847), Colonel of the 72nd Highlanders, who served in the Peninsula and at Waterloo. William Blake, the poet (1757-1827) was baptised in the church.

The church is also the burial place of Beau Brummell's grandparents, William and Jane, who died in the 1770s; "Old Q", the eccentric and rakish Duke of Queensbury (died 1810) and James Gilray the caricaturist (died 1815).

Leave the church by the same entrance and turn right along Jermyn Street.

By the early 19th century Jermyn Street was the location for numerous private hotels and superior lodging houses. Hotels listed in the 1819 *Directory* included Reddish's, Beal's, Batt's, Blake's, Durant's, Millar's and the St. James's.

Paxton & Whitfield, cheesemongers, (no.93), started with a stall in Aldwych Market in 1742 before they moved to Jermyn Street to be near their affluent customers. The building is late 17th century, although the shop front is Victorian.

Floris London (no.89) was established in 1730 and received its first Royal Warrant in 1820. The shop, in a late 17th century building, is fitted out with mahogany showcases from the 1851 Great Exhibition.

Further along on the right you reach the entrance to the modern Piccadilly Arcade with a statue to Beau Brummell erected in 2002. Brummell is credited with the creation of the elegant and restrained masculine dress style of the Regency and the statue shows off his immaculate, yet simple, clothes. Note his tasselled Hessian boots.

Continue along Jermyn Street to the corner of Bury Street.

Here William Brummell kept a lodging house. Through the influence of one of his lodgers, later to become Lord Liverpool, William's son Billy, father of George 'Beau' Brummell, began his rise through society.

Retrace your steps and turn right down Duke Street.

4, Duke Street was home in 1810 to Simon Bolivar, liberator of Latin America. With no immigration controls at the time, England was a refuge for radicals, reformers and political activists from many countries.

Turn right into King Street.

Almack's Assembly Rooms, that cornerstone of Regency Society, opened in 1765 on the site of the present Post-Modern building at nos.26-8 (Almack House). By 1800 it was an exclusive venue for ladies and gentlemen of the upper classes to meet, dance, socialise, see and be seen and was the Marriage Mart *par excellence* for young ladies of breeding. No alcohol was served and the Patronesses, who could blight reputations by refusing to issue a voucher of admission, enforced the strictest of rules. Even the Duke of Wellington was turned away for arriving in trousers and not the requisite knee breeches.

Opposite Almack House is the auction house Christie's, established in 1766.

In contrast to the respectability of Almack's, the warren of courts and passages to the south of King Street were home to the courtesans, the demi-reps and the 'Fashionable Impures' who entertained the gentlemen of St James's. Although Covent Garden was still a notorious area for prostitution, the higher class courtesans went where their clients lived and played and so they established themselves on the doorsteps of the Palace and the elegant homes of St James's.

Turn left from King Street into Crown Passage.

Crown Passage is a narrow alley very evocative of the 18th and 19th centuries and still lit by gas. It retains several 18th century houses and, at no.18, an 18th century shop front. At the end is another *Red Lion* pub, older than the one of the same name in Duke of York Street.

Retrace your steps, turn left into King Street and cross St James's Street into St James's Place.

Member of Parliament William Huskisson lived at 28, St James's Place. On 15th September 1830 the unfortunate man made history by stepping across the tracks at the opening of the Liverpool and Manchester Railway to speak to the Duke of Wellington. He was hit by Stephenson's *Rocket*, becoming the first railway fatality. More romantically, Mary Robinson, the lovely actress known as Perdita, and mistress of both the Prince Regent and Charles James Fox, lived at no.14 in the 1790s.

Many of the houses in the Place are late 17th-18th century in date but they are overshadowed by Spencer House (no.27) which is one of the foremost Georgian houses in London. Built in the 1750s it was remodelled in the 1780s by Henry Holland who was also responsible for Carlton House. It has been magnificently restored and is open to the public on most Sundays.

With your back to Spencer House walk straight ahead and turn left into a very narrow passage just after no.23. Go through into Green Park.

Green Park was the least fashionable of the central London parks during the Regency. A pleasant open space, it was ideal for more informal strolling or riding. Heyer fans will recall Lufra, the uncontrollable hound in *Frederica*, pursuing the herd of cows that were grazed here. For a penny you could buy a cup of milk warm from one of them. Many features have changed since the Regency, but Queen's Walk on the eastern edge, laid out in 1730, remains. The western part was largely open in the early 19th century and there was a pool in the central valley, fed by Tyburn Brook. That was filled in during 1837 and the reservoir to the north east disappeared in 1855.

Walk ends.

Walk 2: Hyde Park & Kensington Gardens

Distance: 2 miles.

Transport: Nearest tube station – Hyde Park Corner. Buses 9, 14, 19, 22, 52, 74, 137, 702.

When to visit: Apsley House opening hours vary throughout the year – do check before planning to visit.

Useful websites:

Apsley House: https://wellingtoncolection.co.uk

Wellington Arch: https://english-heritage.org.uk/visit/places/wellington-arch

Hyde Park: https://royalparks.org.uk/visit/parks/hyde-park

Kensington Palace: https://hrp.org.uk/KensingtonPalace

Start at Hyde Park Corner.

Apsley House – known as Number One London because it was the first house that stage coaches on the Hyde Park turnpike reached after the toll-gate – was built by Robert Adam in the 1770s and purchased by the 1st Marquis Wellesley in 1807. He sold it in 1817 to his brother, the Duke of Wellington, who needed a London residence at the start of his political career.

The interior is beautifully preserved and contains the Duke's collection of art works, and the lavish gifts showered on him by grateful heads of state after the battle of Waterloo and the defeat of Napoleon. A banquet is still held annually on 18th June in the Waterloo Gallery. A visit inside is well worthwhile.

Opposite the house is the Wellington (or Constitution) Arch. (1826-9, although the statue group on top is 1912) It was intended as a great entrance to Buckingham Palace, but proved too much of a bottleneck for carriages. It is possible to climb up inside for a view from the balconies.

Before you go into Hyde Park, turn your back on Apsley House and look diagonally right, across to the Lanesborough Hotel. Between 1766 and 1865 Tattersall's famous auction ring and "grand mart for everything connected with the sports of the field, the business of the turf and equestrian recreations" was situated just behind the old St George's Hospital on this site.

Sales were on Mondays and Thursdays in the winter and Mondays only in the summer. Even on days where there was no sale it was an essential place to meet for every Regency gentleman and for all their hangers-on too. Sir John Lade, the infamous racehorse breeder and whip once drove a coach and four round Tattersall's small enclosed yard for a bet.

The Hyde Park Turnpike gates were removed in 1825 as a hindrance to traffic.

Go through into Hyde Park.

Hyde Park was on the western edge of London during the Regency and development had only just begun to link the villages of Kensington and Knightsbridge to London.

The Picture of London, a guidebook of 1807 from which all the quotations for this walk are taken, remarks that, "a few years since, Hyde Park was a little deficient in wood, many of the old trees having decayed; but recently some judicious plantings have been made that will greatly enliven its general appearance."

Walk as far as the sandy track, turn left and walk along beside it.

This track is Rotten Row – the *Route du Roi*, or King's Route – dating from 1690. During the Season High Society paraded here every afternoon on horseback, in carriages and on foot. It was essential to see and to be seen in your most fashionable clothes. "We recommend [the stranger] to pause at some spot...from which his eye can command the entire picture of carriages, horsemen, and foot passengers, in the park, all eager to push forward in various directions."

Walk along Rotten Row and take the 4th path to the right and then turn left where five paths meet to follow the north bank of the Serpentine (Serpentine Road).

The Serpentine was formed in 1730 by damming the Westbourne, one of London's lost rivers that flows down from Hampstead. Harriet Westbrook, the first wife of poet Percy Bysshe Shelley, drowned herself in the Serpentine in 1816. She had married him when she was just sixteen, was mother to two of his children, but was abandoned by him when he eloped with Mary Godwin in 1814.

"In severe winters, when the Serpentine River is frozen over, the ice is almost covered with people...a number of booths were pitched for the refreshment of the populace; and here and there was a group of six, eight or more, fashionable young men, skating, and describing very difficult figures, in the manner of a country dance, with particular neatness and facility of execution... From the number of accidents which happen annually on this river when frozen over, his Majesty gave the Humane Society a spot of ground on its bank on which they have erected a most convenient receiving-house for the recovery of the apparently drowned; it cost upwards of £500." Devices to puff tobacco smoke into the rectum in an attempt to revive drowning victims were provided by the Humane Society and placed at strategic locations. They seem unlikely to have been effective.

The Serpentine Drive joins the West Carriage Drive and curves round to cross the bridge (1825-8). Just before the curve on the right is a powder magazine (1805), now the Serpentine Gallery North.

The Picture of London describes "a powder magazine and a guardroom, both of brick, the sight of which if they must be there for the sake of any convenience, ought to be obscured by planting.... Hyde Park is used for the field days of the horse and foot guards...and for some martial reviews; which however is not mentioned as an advantage to the beauty of the place, as these exercises destroy the verdure of the park." The powder magazine is now a restaurant.

Cross the bridge and take the first path on the right.

You are now in Kensington Gardens. The lake on the right, formed by joining up small ponds along the course of the Westbourne River, is known as the Long Water.

Follow the path to the head of the Long Water.

Between Bayswater Road (the Uxbridge Turnpike road in the early 19th century) and the head of the Long Water are Italian Gardens created at the behest of Prince Albert. At the beginning of the 19th century the area was very different. "Beneath a row of trees, running parallel with the keeper's garden, are two springs, greatly resorted to; one is mineral, and is drank; the other is used to bathe weak eyes with. At the former, in fine weather, sits a woman with a table and chairs, and glasses for the accommodation of visitors. People of fashion often go in their carriages... and send their servants with jugs for the water...The brim of the further spring is frequently surrounded by persons, chiefly of the lower order, bathing their eyes." A bench on the east side of the Italian Gardens marks the site.

Take Budge's Walk, the path striking diagonally south west across Kensington Gardens towards the Round Pond, then turn right following the edge of the Pond, and take the linking path to the Broad Walk in front of the Palace.

"Numbers of people of fashion, mingled with a great multitude of well-dressed persons of various ranks, crowd the walk for many hours together... No servant in livery, nor women with pattens [wooden or metal overshoes], nor persons carrying bundles, are admitted into the gardens."

Despite this charming scene, the guide book warns, "It is not always safe to be in Hyde Park or Kensington Gardens, after dark. These places being so extensive, opportunities of robbery, or ill-usage, are easily given; and it is impossible to shut out public robbers or other ill-disposed persons."

At the Broad Walk turn right and immediately left to get to the entrance to Kensington Palace.

At the Palace there are royal staterooms to see, a collection of court dress in all its complexity and the room where Princess Victoria heard that she had become queen – the end of the Georgian era.

Walk ends.

Walk 3: Mayfair North

Distance: 2.75 miles.

Transport: Nearest tube station – Hyde Park Corner. Buses 9, 14, 19, 22, 52, 74, 137, 702.

When to visit: Monday to Saturday for shopping. See Royal Institution website for opening hours. (Normally 9-5 on weekdays).

Useful website:

Royal Institution: https://www.rigb.org/

Start at Hyde Park Corner, enter Hyde Park and walk north along the edge of the park to the Achilles statue, just past the Queen Elizabeth gates.

The Achilles statue was erected in 1822 in honour of the Duke of Wellington. It was the first public nude statue in England and caused an outcry, with ladies of delicate sensibilities taking alternative routes to avoid seeing it. A Cruickshank cartoon of 1822, with the caption, "Ladies buy your leaf", shows sniggering women ogling the figure with its skimpy fig leaf.

Leave the Park into Park Lane by the Queen Elizabeth gates.

A statue of Byron is on your right, stranded on a traffic island. At the time of writing there are hopes that it might be moved.

Turn left, pass the bus stops. Go under Park Lane by the subway. Turn left up Park Lane, turn right into Curzon Street then left into South Audley Street.

Note the handsome 18th century ironwork in front of the houses opposite South Audley street, including conical snuffers for the 'links' or flaming torches carried by link boys and used to guide people home at night.

Walk up South Audley Street on the left hand side.

Charles X, the last Bourbon King of France (1757-1836), lived at no.72 from 1805 until 1814 when the royal family came out of exile and returned to France. Charles succeeded to the throne after the death of his brother Louis XVIII in 1824.

No.77 is the site of Alderman Wood's house where Queen Caroline resided on her return from Italy in 1820. She would show herself from the balcony to enthusiastic crowds – much to the fury of her estranged husband George IV.

On the right-hand side of the street is Grosvenor Chapel, an example of the 18th century 'chapels of ease' built to serve the upper class inhabitants of the new Mayfair streets and squares. The speculative builders made a return from the rents for the private pews.

Opposite the Chapel is Aldford Street. In 1811 Harriet Westbrook, Shelley's first wife, eloped with him from no.23 when she was just sixteen. She drowned herself in the Serpentine in 1816. In that year Beau Brummell moved to no.13.

On the corner of South Audley Street and Mount Street is Purdey's, the gunsmiths, founded in 1814. James Purdey had worked for the iconic Manton brothers as chief stocker, or maker of the gunstocks, and no gentleman who could afford it during the Regency would be without guns from one or both of these makers. The firm moved here in 1881.

At Mount Street retrace your steps along South Audley Street and turn left into Hill Street.

A significant number of 18th century houses survive in Hill Street. The "hill" names in this area refer to the slopes down to Tyburn Brook which still runs beneath the pavements.

Turn right down Chesterfield Hill which retains several houses dating from the 1750s. Some have charming balconies, for example, nos. 12 & 15. Note Hay's Mews crossing the street – this would have provided stabling for the many horses and carriages kept by the fashionable occupants of the surrounding houses.

At the end turn right into Charles Street and then left into Chesterfield Street.

Chesterfield Street is completely Georgian in appearance, although some buildings lost in the Blitz have been rebuilt (eg no.6). Most date from 1755. No.10 is from 1795 and no.1a is early 19th century.

Beau Brummell lived at no.4 from his arrival in London in 1799 until his debts forced him to move. His narrow house is hardly changed in appearance and it is easy to imagine the Beau spending the entire morning getting dressed – with an admiring audience of the Dandy Set – and then setting forth about noon. If the weather was inclement he would take a sedan chair – he considered a hackney carriage to be unsuitable transport for a gentleman.

Walk down to Curzon Street.

As you stand at the entrance to Curzon Street and look right you would have seen, until 1937, Chesterfield House whose grounds occupied the entire northern block up to South Audley Street. Opposite remain some grand Georgian houses – this was a very smart street indeed.

The bluestocking Berry sisters, Mary and Agnes, lived at no.8 where Mary pursued a career as an author and editor and they held their fashionable intellectual salons. Both women and men, including the

Duke of Wellington, visited them in large numbers. As the evening drew on Mary would order their servant, "No more petticoats," at which point he would extinguish the porch light. No ladies would call after that, but gentlemen knew they would still be admitted.

Turn left into Curzon Street past the Saudi Arabian Embassy which occupies Crewe House.

Crewe House was begun in the mid-18th century and is a fine example of a London mansion, although the presence of armed policemen makes stopping to admire it rather difficult.

Opposite was the Mayfair Chapel, a notorious 'marriage shop' for clandestine unions until the Hardwicke Marriage Act of 1754 put a stop to them. George II was rumoured to have married Hannah Lightfoot there in 1759. The chapel survived until the late 19th century.

Follow the street until it bends sharply left. At the bend go straight ahead into Landsdowne Row, cross Berkeley Street into Hay Hill, up Hay Hill then left into Grafton Street.

Grafton Street was begun in 1769, one of the last of the 18th century developments in the area. A number of good houses of the period remain.

Walk along Grafton Street and turn right into Albemarle Street. Walk down as far as the Royal Institution.

At no.23 was Alfred's Club. Described as "the dullest place in existence" by the Earl of Dudley, it still numbered Byron amongst its members.

More lively would have been The Royal Institution of Great Britain at no.21, dedicated to the "diffusion of knowledge, and facilitating the general introduction of useful mechanical improvements." Visitors were kept warm by the latest heating innovations of Count Rumford, adventurer and inventor. Lectures there were so popular, and Albemarle Street became so jammed with traffic as a result, that it was turned into the first one-way street in London. The Royal Institution can be visited and includes the Faraday Museum.

Return to Grafton Street, turn right and walk along to New Bond Street then turn left.

New Bond Street is the continuation north of Old Bond Street. The stretch from Old Bond Street to Clifford Street was built up by 1700 and the rest up to Oxford Street after 1716.

Virtually nothing remains earlier than the mid-19th century but, despite the physical changes, it retains its character as a highly exclusive shopping street, just as it was throughout the Regency. Along with its southern extension it was a fashionable 'lounge' for the beau monde, particularly in the afternoon.

Steven's and Long's hotels were both patronised by the *ton*. Byron and Scott dined at Long's and Steven's was a home from home for aristocratic army officers. Captain Gronow records that, if a stranger wished to dine at Steven's, the staff would inform him blandly that there were no tables, whether there were or not.

Not everyone was of the highest refinement, however. The eccentric Lord Camelford lived over a grocer's shop at the site of no.148 (now The Fine Arts Society), and provoked a riot in 1801 when London was illuminated to celebrate the short-lived peace. He refused to allow his landlord to light up the windows and the house was attacked by a mob, during the course of which his lordship threw one man down the stairs and went out into the street armed with a cudgel to repel all comers. He was killed in a duel some years later and died forgiving his opponent.

In 1797 Lord Nelson lived next door in a house on the site of no.147 after losing his right arm at the battle of Cape St Vincent. He was in continuous pain at the time and was nursed devotedly by Lady Nelson who attended every dressing of the wound until she felt capable of doing it herself.

The shop front of what was Savory & Moore (no.143) is early 19th century. The firm was founded in 1794. Customers included Wellington and Lady Hamilton (who lived in New Bond Street after Nelson's death). The Duke of Sussex, brother of George IV, often dined there with Thomas Field Savory, a talented chemist. In 1815 Savory acquired the patent for Seidlitz powders, the internationally popular laxative of the time, and became a very wealthy man as a result.

Turn round at no.143 and retrace your steps, turn left into Conduit Street and left again into St George Street.

There are 18th century houses to be found in St George Street. Continue up to St George's church, a highly fashionable location for Regency weddings and usually referred to as St George's, Hanover Square, although it is not actually on the square itself. The interior retains many Georgian features, although the height of the box pews was greatly reduced in the 1870s. The Earl of Jersey was a church warden here in 1794. His wife, the Countess of Jersey, was one of the Patronesses of Almack's and was nicknamed Silence because of her never-ending chatter.

Leave the church and cross into Maddox Street, go along it and right into New Bond Street. Walk north and turn left into Brook Street.

Brook Street contains a large number of 18th and early 19th century houses which give a good impression of its appearance during the Regency. Note particularly 25, 39, 66, 68, 72, 76 and 86.

Turn left into Grosvenor Square and walk down the eastern side to Grosvenor Street.

Grosvenor Square is the largest square in Mayfair and was developed in 1725, although nothing now remains that a Regency Londoner would recognise. The square was not gas-lit until 1842 because of opposition by the highly influential residents who preferred the flambeaux fixed outside their front doors.

At no.44 was the house where, in 1820, the Cato Street conspirators intended to blow up all the ministers of the Crown while they were dining with Lord Harrowby. Their plan was that this would trigger a popular uprising and the Bank of England and the Tower of London would be seized. The conspirators were betrayed, found guilty of high treason and hanged.

Turn left into Grosvenor Street.

Grosvenor Street also has several 18th century houses. Note no.34 with its flambeaux snuffers and original window-blind boxes.

Turn left into Davies Street, then right into Brook Street and left into South Molton Street. Walk along to Oxford Street.

South Molton Street is also on the line of Tyburn Brook. Nos.14-26 are 18th century. Poet and visionary artist William Blake lived at no.17 (1804-20) and Miss Macdonald, a fashionable modiste, had her shop at no.50.

Walk ends at Oxford Street.

Walk 4: Piccadilly & Mayfair South

Distance: 2 miles.

Transport: Nearest tube station – Piccadilly Circus. Buses 12, 139, 14, 19, 29, 453, 9, 88, 94.

When to visit: Many shops will be closed on Sunday although the Burlington Arcade is open. The Royal Academy is closed on Mondays.

Useful websites:

Royal Academy of Arts: https://www.royalacademy.org.uk/

Burlington Arcade: https://www.burlingtonarcade.com/

Start at Piccadilly Circus and walk along the northern (right) side of Piccadilly. After Sackville Street watch out for the entrance to Albany on your right.

It is possible to go into the forecourt of these exclusive residences. Albany was built in 1770 and converted in 1804 into chambers for single gentlemen who needed a London *pied à terre*. Byron was a resident for a while and Jane Austen's banker brother Henry had his office in one of the single-storey courtyard buildings. More recently, when ladies were admitted, Georgette Heyer lived here, close to the characters of her novels.

Turn right out of Albany and almost immediately right into the courtyard of Burlington House.

The home of the Royal Academy of Arts, Burlington House was begun in 1704. The main block facing you was altered by Campbell c.1718 in the Palladian style. Lord George Cavendish bought the house in 1815.

Later it was sold to the government who leased it to the Royal Academy. The two side wings were added in the 1870s.

Go back into Piccadilly, turn right and almost immediately right again to the entrance of Burlington Arcade. Do not enter the Arcade yet. Cross Piccadilly to the south side.

Hatchard's bookshop was established at no.187 in 1797, although the building and shop front are more modern. It is the only remaining bookshop out of a number mentioned in an 1807 guidebook. "English booksellers' shops, which are frequented as lounging shops, and which are provided with all new publications, newspapers etc, are Ridgeway's, Stockdale's and Hatchard's."

Almost next door is the even older firm of Fortnum and Mason's, started in 1707 by a royal footman and his landlord. Many Peninsula war officers, including the Duke of Wellington, would buy hampers of provisions here to equip themselves before they went on campaign.

A little further along at no.170-3 is the site of Bullock's Museum or The Egyptian Hall. Erected in 1812, in 1815 it was exhibiting Napoleon's fabulously equipped carriage, captured after Waterloo. As one guidebook of the time said, "It is impossible to refer to this acquisition without feeling a patriotic exultation" – which may have been somewhat dampened after viewing the rest of the vast collection which included "amphibious animals in great variety, several mummies and non-descript animals, bones etc." It was demolished in 1905.

Cross Piccadilly to the Burlington Arcade entrance.

Burlington Arcade is a covered street of luxury shops built as part of Lord George Cavendish's remodelling of Burlington House. It was opened in 1819. The façade onto Piccadilly is early 20th century, but the remainder is original. Until recently the Arcade was still patrolled by its top-hatted and uniformed beadles whose duty was to enforce suitably genteel behaviour.

Walk up the Burlington Arcade (If closed, walk past the entrance and take the first right into Old Bond Street), turn left into Burlington Gardens and then left into Old Bond Street. Cross the street, walk down the right-hand side to the Royal Arcade.

Old Bond Street was developed from 1684 onwards and from the 18th century has been one of the premier shopping streets for luxury goods in London. No buildings of the period remain, but the ambiance of luxury and wealth would be very familiar to a returning Regency lady.

Priscilla Wakefield observed in 1814, "Bond-street is the grand mart for fashionable items of dress, and is consequently the resort of ladies of the *ton*, who assemble there in splendid carriages; whilst idle beaux, distinguished by the appellation of Loungers come to gaze at them, and, in their turn to attract attention."

Two until five was the most fashionable time to be seen here during the Season and Sir Walter Scott, Byron, Brummell and the Prince Regent were frequently to be observed. On one occasion politician Charles James Fox laid a wager with the Prince – on which side of the street would most cats be found? The Prince bet on the shady side, but Fox won by choosing the sunshine.

It is not recorded whether they visited the exhibition in 1799 of Oliver Cromwell's embalmed head at Mead Court, "where the rattlesnake was shown last year". One sympathises with the neighbours.

Striking a rather higher moral tone was Hookham's library at no.15, opposite Stafford Street, one of the smartest of the numerous bookshops and lending libraries in the street. Next door at no.14 are the art dealers, Colnaghi. They have been in Old Bond Street only since 1911, but the firm originated in London in 1783 when Paul Colnaghi ignored

Benjamin Franklin's advice to emigrate to America and instead set up an art gallery and print publishing business. Between 1792-7 they published the best-selling *Cries of London* prints and then, on the death of Nelson, were ready to exploit the national mood with a portrait engraving.

No.13 was Gentleman John Jackson's gymnasium where he taught boxing and fencing to the gentlemen of the *ton* and even gave the Prince Regent lessons.

On either side of the entrance to the Royal Arcade (1879) are the sites of two significant Regency shops. Gieves the tailors, at no.27, made uniforms for all the naval heroes of the Napoleonic wars – Nelson, Hood, Rodney, Howe – and the records and measurements were preserved until they were destroyed during the Second World War. Dollands, at no.28, supplied Nelson with the telescope used on the *Victory*. The Duke of Wellington also bought his telescopes from Dolland. The superior tailor Weston was at no.37.

Trufitt & Hill (no.23), had been operating in Old Bond Street since 1805 when Francis Trufitt set up at no.40 as 'court hair and head dresser'. They were wigmakers to George IV. No lady would visit a hairdresser's shop, however: she would receive visits at home.

Turn into the Royal Arcade, go through into Albemarle Street. Turn left and walk down towards Piccadilly. (On Sundays go past the Arcade, turn left into Stafford Street and then left into Albemarle Street).

Virtually every literary 'name' of the 19th century must have come to Albemarle Street to visit the publisher John Murray. The firm moved to no.50 in 1812 and has been there ever since. Amongst the greats, Murray published Jane Austen and Lord Byron and, at Byron's wish, burned his diaries after his death.

The street had at least three fashionable hotels in the Regency period, including the Lothian and the Clarendon. The most famous was Grillon's opposite John Murray's. Louis XVIII stayed there in 1814 during the somewhat premature celebrations of Napoleon's defeat.

Guests could have borrowed books from "Earle's original French, English, Spanish and Italian circulating library...now removed to No.47, Albemarle-street, Piccadilly, where all new books in the instructive and entertaining classes of literature are constantly added..."

Retrace your steps, turn left into Stafford Street to Dover Street and turn left again.

The 17th century building on the northern corner was the *Duke of Albemarle* pub. At no.6 Dover Street (just before the *Clarence* pub) leading gunsmith Joseph Manton had his shop and shooting gallery, established 1810, where gentlemen went to 'culp a wafer' with a well-placed shot. His improvements to duelling pistols would have been appreciated by many of the bucks and rakes of the day.

Turn around and walk back up Dover Street, then turn left into Hay Hill.

Hay Hill was a farm on the banks of the Eye Brook, a tributary of the Tyburn. The Prince Regent and some companions were set upon by footpads here and robbed of two shillings and sixpence.

Turn right into Berkeley Street and first right into Bruton Lane which follows the line of the Eye Brook that still runs under your feet.

In the early 19th century it was South Bruton Mews and the strange kink on its course marks a large block of stables and carriage houses, fitting into the junction between the Berkeley estate and the Conduit Mead estate.

Cross Bruton Street and enter Bruton Place.

Bruton Place was a mews. Georgian houses survive at nos.1-7.

Walk along Bruton Place to emerge into Berkeley Square.

Berkeley Square was developed from the end of the 17th century. In the Regency the south side was taken up by the gardens of Landsdown House which stretched down to Piccadilly and Devonshire House. On the west side is a series of 1740s houses with magnificent original ironwork.

No.50 in the south-west corner was the home of George Canning. He was Foreign Secretary in 1809 when he had a major dispute with Lord Castlereagh over the deployment of troops to the continent. When Castlereagh discovered that Canning was plotting to have him replaced as Secretary of War by Lord Wellesley he challenged him to a duel, creating a political scandal. Canning, who had never fired a pistol before, was wounded in the thigh. He was briefly Prime Minister before his death in 1827.

There was an equestrian statue of George III in the centre of the square until the horse's legs collapsed in 1827.

The south-east corner of the square was the location of Gunter's tea shop where exquisite ices and sorbets could be eaten, either in the shop or in one's carriage under the shade of the great plane trees, planted 1789 and still standing.

Leave the square in the south-west corner straight down into Fitzmaurice Place, leading into Curzon Street and then second left into Bolton Street.

Until 1708 Bolton Street marked the western limit of London. Some late 18th century houses survive on the east side.

The novelist and playwright Fanny Burney (Madame d'Arblay) lived in a house on the site of no.11. Her first three novels – *Evelina, Cecilia* and

Camilla – were huge critical and popular successes and she was taken up by Dr Johnson. She followed her husband to France when he took a post with Bonaparte and remained there for ten years. In 1811 she underwent a mastectomy for breast cancer, without anaesthetic, and wrote on the subject. Her final novel, *The Wanderer or Female Difficulties*, was published in 1814.

Two significant Regency landmarks were situated at the Piccadilly end of Bolton Street. On one corner was the Pulteney Hotel where many of the visiting royals, including the Russian Emperor Alexander, were lodged during the Allied celebrations of peace in 1814. The emperor's sister spoke with appreciation of the innovative flush toilets, a great novelty in a hotel.

On the other corner was Watier's, the 'Dandy Club', established 1807 on the suggestion of the Prince Regent by his chef, Jean-Baptise Watier. George was tired of the monotonous boiled fowl and beefsteaks in oyster sauce served by the majority of clubs. With Brummell as perpetual president, standards of dress and behaviour were high and fortunes were won and lost at the high-stakes macao tables. By 1819 it was in decline and had lost its exclusivity.

Turn right into Piccadilly and first right into Clarges Street.

This street retains a number of 18th century houses on its west side, including the home of Charles James Fox at no.46. Fox was a fiery politician who spent most of his career in opposition and was one of the most colourful characters of the early Regency period. He was an opponent of slavery and a supporter of both the French revolution and American independence. His private life was a public scandal – he was bankrupted twice with gambling debts, was a heavy drinker and womaniser and finally married Elizabeth Armistead, a former mistress of the Prince Regent.

Turn left into Curzon Street and then first left into Half Moon Street. Turn left and walk down to Piccadilly.

Named after the tavern that used to stand on the corner with Piccadilly, Half Moon Street was the first London home of Hero and Sherry in Heyer's *Friday's Child*. It retains many 18th century houses. The gates into Green Park opposite the end of Half Moon Street are c.1735 but were only placed here in 1921.

Turn right into Piccadilly.

At no.94 is Egremont House, built in the 1760, then occupied by the Duke of Cambridge and known as Cambridge House, and for a time the residence of Lord Palmerston. Palmerston entered Parliament as a Tory in 1807 and was hardly out of office until his death in 1865, despite changing parties in the 1830s. He became Secretary at War in 1809 and held that post for twenty years. The house stood empty for many years and, at the time of writing, is being redeveloped as a hotel and private residences.

Take the first right into White Horse Street.

Named for another Piccadilly tavern, White Horse Street's twists reflect the line of Tyburn Brook.

Follow White Horse Street into Shepherd's Market.

Shepherd's Market was built in the 1740s to supply food to the developing Mayfair area. It was built on the site of the riotous old St James's May Fair that was finally suppressed in the 1760s. The present market hall is a mid-19th century building, but the area is still characterful and has many places to eat.

From Shepherd's Market take Shepherd Street in the south west corner and turn left into Hertford Street.

Hertford Street has many medium-sized houses from the 1760s and 70s. The dramatist Richard Brinsley Sheridan lived at no.10 (1795-1802). Author of such major plays as *School For Scandal* and *The Critics*, he was also a Whig politician and sat in Parliament for over twenty years. He died, impoverished, in 1816.

At the end of Hertford Street turn left into Old Park Lane and down to Piccadilly where the **Walk ends.**

Walk 5: Soho North

Distance: 2 miles.

Transport: Nearest tube station – Tottenham Court Road. Buses 19, 38, 55, 73, 98, 390.

When to visit: At any time, although Monday-Saturday for shopping.

Useful website:

St Anne's church: https://www.stannes-soho.org.uk/

Start at Tottenham Court tube station. Walk up Oxford Street on the right hand side and pause at Berner's Street or *take the 55 or 98 bus to the Wardour Street stop on Oxford Street and cross the road to Berner's Street.*

No original buildings remain in Berner's Street but it was at the heart of the artistic quarter during the late 18th and early 19th century. Artists John Opie and Henry Fuseli and architects Sir Robert Smirke, Sir William Chambers and Thomas Hardwick were all residents. Poet Samuel Taylor Coleridge lived at no.71 (1812-16).

It is best known for the Berner's Street Hoax. Theodore Hook, apparently as a result of a bet to make an ordinary house the most famous in England, sent out thousands of letters and orders under the name of the unfortunate Mrs Tottenham who lived at no.54. On 27th November 1810 the street was a scene of utter chaos with hundreds of tradesmen delivering everything from coffins to coal. Numerous dignitaries, including the Lord Mayor and the Governor of the Bank of England, called on the poor lady.

Continue along Oxford Street and cross to Marks & Spencer on the south side of the road.

M&S is on the site of the Pantheon, built in 1772 for masquerades, assemblies and concerts, including the scandalous Cyprians' (Prostitutes') Balls. These functions, often illustrated by Rowlandson, continued after it was rebuilt following a fire in 1792. It became the short-lived English Opera House in 1813 before it was closed down by the Lord Chamberlain for immorality. Eventually, in 1833, it became the popular Pantheon Bazaar, finally demolished in 1937.

Turn and walk back along Oxford Street and turn right into Poland Street to enter the Soho district.

The long streets and grid pattern of this part of London reflect the fields that were here before the area was developed in the 17th century. Quite a few street names have changed since the Regency and the old ones are given in brackets.

Walk down Poland Street and pause outside the *King's Arms*, built on the site of the pub where the Ancient Order of Druids was re-formed in 1781. Diagonally across Great Marlborough Street is no.15 where Shelley had lodgings for a few months in 1811 when he was sent down from Oxford University. Apparently, as a supporter of Polish freedom, he was attracted by the street name.

Singer Elizabeth Billington – known as the Poland Street Mantrap – mistress of the Duke of Rutland and George, Prince of Wales, lived at no.54 until 1792. William Blake lived at no.28 (1785-1791) and printed his *Songs of Innocence* here. Near the end of the street is the early 19th century *Star & Garter* pub.

At the end of Poland Street, at the junction with Broadwick Street, look to your left. Here was the pump where Dr John Snow made the link between polluted water supply and cholera in 1854. Although later than our period, this is a reminder of just how dangerous life in 19th century London was.

Turn right into Broadwick Street (was Broad Street) and then right into Marshall Street.

Marshall Street was developed in the early 18th century on the site of a Great Plague mass-burial pit. Walk up it to Ganton Street: the houses diagonally opposite, north of the junction, were built in the 1820s on the site of the Carnaby Market

Turn left into Ganton Street and right into Newburgh Street.

Newburgh Street has some original shop fronts at nos.5 and 6.

Turn left at the end of Newburgh Street into Foubert's Place, following the line of the edge of the market, and left again into Carnaby Street.

Carnaby Street retains many of the attractive little 1820s market-infill shops and houses at its northern end. This area housed Huguenot refugees in the 17th century and remained very much a quarter for shopkeepers and tradesmen in the 19th century.

At the end of Carnaby Street turn left into Beak Street (was Silver Street).

In Beak Street stay on the right-hand side to Great Pulteney Street, then look across to see the row of early 18th century houses opposite with their early 19th century shop fronts (nos.65 onwards), interrupted by the startling 1847 pub front at no.75.

Walk along to Lexington Street (was Little Windmill Street) and turn right to Brewer Street.

At the junction with Brewer Street you can see Great Windmill Street curving away on the line of a track from what is now Piccadilly Circus to the windmill that stood in the fields close by.

Turn right and cross the road to peer through the bars of the gate at 45A. A late 19th century stables with ramps and carriage houses marks the high point of the reign of the horse in London.

Turn and walk back eastwards along Brewer Street (was Little Pulteney Street). At the end turn right into Wardour Street and continue down to the gardens and forbidding frontage of St Anne's church on your left.

The seats in St Anne's churchyard are a good place to sit and rest. This was the main burial place for the Soho area from the 1630s to the mid 19th century and it is no wonder the ground is so raised – an estimated 100,000 people were buried in three quarters of an acre of ground here.

Retrace your steps up Wardour Street and turn right into Old Compton Street (was Compton Street).

Old Compton Street was the heart of the French community during the 18th and 19th centuries and has always been full of shops and restaurants.

Walk along to Greek Street and turn left.

Greek Street has had some notable residents including Casanova in 1764 and Thomas de Quincy, author of *Confessions of an Opium-Eater*, who ran away from school to seedy lodgings here in 1802. Walk up the west side and look across to no.21 with its early 19th century shop front. Next to it, no.20, retains the iron hoist from the original colourman's shop.

Cross Bateman Street and look across to Wedgwood Mews.

This was built as a house in the late 17th century and subdivided in the early 19th century. Josiah Wedgwood had his showrooms here from 1774 until 1795 when he moved to St James's Square.

Cross the road and go right through the arch by what was the Pillars of Hercules pub into Manette Street.

The late 18th century St Anne's parish workhouse is just past the chapel on the left hand side.

Return to Greek Street, turn right and into Soho Square.

On your right on the corner is the House of St Barnabus, one of the finest in Soho. It was built in 1746 and occupied by Richard Beckford, one of the Jamaica sugar magnates and slave owners. It was let to the Westminster Commission of Sewers in 1811 and eventually became the office of Sir Joseph William Bazalgette who revolutionised London's sewers after the Great Stink of 1858. The sign "House of Charity" on the Soho Square face of the house relates to its function from 1861 when it described itself as an institution where men, women and children of all walks of life, were able to "apply for aid without a loss of self-respect".

Turn left into Soho Square, go around the corner and then left into Carlisle Street and right into Dean Street.

At no.6 Dean Street you can see the back of 4-6 Soho Square which was Trotter's or, The Soho Bazaar, a covered market built in 1816 for people thrown out of work during the post-Napoleonic war slump, especially women. It had two floors of stalls and counters and was very successful.

Turn and walk back along Dean Street, crossing Carlisle Street.

Next to the *Nellie Dean* pub at no.88 is a fine Rococo shop front, one of the very few in London. Continuing along Dean Street look up to see a nice modern inn sign for the *Crown & Two Chairmen* pub on the left just before Bateman Street – a reminder of the sedan chairs that plied these streets.

Turn left into Old Compton Street and left again into Frith Street.

Many of the old houses remain here, hidden behind later fronts, although a nice Gothic shop front of 1816 can be seen at no.15.

Artist John Constable lodged in Frith Street (1810-11) and the actor William Macready was at no.64 in 1816. After the junction with Bateman Street there is a good row, nos.58-60, with handsome door cases and ironwork. Opposite, no.6, was William Hazlitt's house in 1830. He died here in 1830 with Charles Lamb at his bedside.

Turn left into Soho Square and continue round clockwise, crossing Carlisle Street.

33-35 Soho Square, now modern buildings, was the site of naturalist Sir Joseph Banks' house. 4-6 was Trotter's Bazaar.

Turn left into Soho Street and back to Oxford Street.

Walk ends.

Walk 6: Soho South to Somerset House

Distance: 2.5 miles.

Transport: Nearest tube station – Leicester Square. Buses 24, 29, 176.

When to visit: For shopping, Monday-Saturday. Franklin's house is closed Monday-Thursday. It is open for an architectural tour on Fridays and a "Historical experience" on Saturdays and Sundays.

Useful websites:

Church of Notre Dame: https://www.ndfchurch.org/a-propos/

Benjamin Franklin's House: https://benjaminfranklinhouse.org/

Somerset House tours: https://www.somersethouse.org.uk/whats-on/historical-highlights-tour

Start from Leicester Square tube, walk west down Cranbourn Street towards Leicester Square, turning right into Leicester Court just before you reach the square. Cross Lisle Street and continue into Newport Place, then left into Gerrard Street.

Gerrard Street is now at the heart of China Town, but during the Regency it was full of coffee houses, taverns and lodgings for writers, artists, architects and actors, such as John Sell Cotman and Charles Kemble.

On the right hand side as you walk along the street is no.9, now a Chinese supermarket. This was the noted *Turk's Head* coffee house, built in 1759, where Dr Johnson and Joshua Reynolds were among the regular visitors. Go inside and through to the back to climb the early 18th century staircase and imagine the cream of Georgian artists and intellectuals who have done the same. (If it is closed, or the staircase is not accessible, it can be seen here https://www.british-history.ac.uk/survey-london/vols33-4/plate-64). The ugly portico dates from 1825 when it became Westminster General Dispensary.

A little further along on the same side no.12 was *Mill's* coffee house (1702-1811).

At the end turn left into Wardour Street (the southern half was called Prince's Street until the late 19th century.)

Wardour Street was known for its antique shops during the Regency. Thomas Sheraton the furniture designer lived at no.103 (1793-5) and no.147 (1798-1800).

Turn left into Lisle St and walk along as far as Leicester Place.

Standing at the Leicester Place junction you have a good view of the northern central side of Lisle Street with its well-preserved row of houses dating to 1791. Walk a little further along to nos.34-5 on the right which have genuine shop fronts of the same date.

Retrace your steps and turn left down Leicester Place (shown on the cover).

Mr Barker's Panorama, "a triumph of perspective," was situated on your left. In 1807 he was showing views of Edinburgh and Gibraltar on two floors of a rotunda 27 metres in diameter. The rotunda itself has been incorporated into the Church of Notre Dame, entered at 5, Leicester Place.

Continue to Leicester Square to the start of the path cutting diagonally across the gardens.

Leicester Square today would be unrecognisable to a Regency Londoner. In the 18th century it was lined with aristocratic houses and the homes of leading artists such as Sir Joshua Reynolds and Hogarth. By the early 19th century shops and places of entertainment had begun to creep in, including a bagnio (bath house and brothel) and Brunet's Hotel (from 1800). Whilst in the square one might also visit the Invisible Girl. 'Trapped' in a glass sphere she would tell the audience, who had paid 2s 6d admission (about £7 now), what they were holding in their hands, answer questions and breathe on them.

Follow the diagonal path across the garden to the south west corner and enter Panton Street.

Panton Street was at the centre of a violent storm in June 1803 when an electrified cloud descended into the street forming a pit and giving off alarming sulphurous smells. Cross Whitcomb Street to the *Tom Cribb* pub, a friendly place for a drink, snack and comfort stop away from the commercialism of Leicester Square.

Tom Cribb, the undefeated bare-knuckle boxing champion of England 1806-28, was landlord here (1812-39) until debt forced him to sell up. It was then called the *Union Arms*. The brewer's sign by the door stating that the building appears to be 'early 20th century' is incorrect – it is the original early 19th century pub, although with a late Victorian bar and frontage.

Continue to Haymarket and turn right, keeping on the right hand side.

Haymarket, as its name suggests, was the main market for hay and straw, serving the numerous stables in the area and the Royal Mews (where Trafalgar Square now is) until 1830. Throughout the 19th century it was much frequented by prostitutes who became known as 'Haymarket Ware'.

Just before the turning into Coventry Street is the oldest remaining shop front in London at nos.33-4. Now a souvenir shop, it was originally tobacconist Fribourg & Treyer's from 1751 and their sign is still on one pane of window glass. Enter to see original 18th century shelving on the right behind the counter and a pretty screen in the Adam style.

Turn back down Haymarket and walk to the Theatre Royal.

The present theatre was built by John Nash in 1820-1 on the site of previous theatres. In 1805 an earlier building was surrounded by a mob when a play called *The Tailors* offended some of the audience. In 1810 the wealthy and eccentric dandy Benjamin Coates hired it for one night so he could play Romeo. He was ever afterwards known as Romeo Coates.

Cross Haymarket to Charles II Street opposite the theatre.

Charles II Street was opened up at this end in the 1820s to give a clear view from St James's Square to the new theatre.

On the left side of Charles II Street turn into the Royal Opera Arcade.

The Royal Opera Arcade is the oldest shopping arcade in Britain, built 1816-18 by Nash and Repton. The interior remains intact except for the loss of the shops on part of the left side where only fronts remain. It is sadly neglected now, with many shops vacant. Walk down, imagining the shallow bow windows full of everything a Regency shopper could desire, and pause at the back entrance to Her Majesty's Theatre.

The current building dates from 1897 but a series of theatres have stood on the site. The one Regency theatregoers would have known – The Opera House – had the first horseshoe-shaped auditorium in Britain and a separate assembly room. *The Picture of London* (1807) describes a glittering interior with tiers of boxes decorated with cherubs, leopards and griffins and a stage eighty feet wide. The season ran from December until June or July.

Walk to the end of the Arcade and turn left into Pall Mall. At the foot of Haymarket cross into Pall Mall East and turn left into Suffolk Street.

Suffolk Street (then Great Suffolk Street) lost its southern end when Pall Mall East was driven through to meet Trafalgar Square. The houses north of Suffolk Place are all that remains, south of Oxford Circus, of Nash's rebuilding during the Regent's Street development. On both sides there are virtually intact 1820s houses and at the far end on the west side is the back of the Theatre Royal, including a very tall and narrow door to bring in scenery.

The Marquess of Winchilsea was living at no.7 when the Duke of Wellington challenged him to a duel in 1829. The marquess had verbally attacked Wellington, then Prime Minister, who was trying to get the Catholic Emancipation Act passed. They met at dawn in Battersea Park. Wellington shot a hole in Winchilsea's coat and the Marquess deloped (fired wide). Honour was satisfied.

Return to Pall Mall East, cross it, and the paved area, go directly ahead and over Cockspur Street to the far side.

At an angle to your right as you stand in front of the Thai restaurant (Norway House) is Warwick House Street, the remains of Warwick Street. Princess Charlotte was made to reside here in Warwick House by her father, the Prince Regent, who wished to separate her from the influence of her mother, his estranged wife Princess Caroline. On July 16th 1814 Charlotte left the house, crossed Cockspur Street, hailed the first hackney carriage she saw and escaped to her mother.

Walk eastwards along Cockspur Street to the southern edge of Trafalgar Square, skirt the lower edge of the square and into the Strand. Turn second right into Craven Street.

Once down the modern steps you are into an almost uninterrupted stretch of 18th century houses, preserved when they were bought up for an extension to Charing Cross Station that never occurred.

On the left, no.36, was the residence of Benjamin Franklin (1757-75). It is open to the public. (Limited hours, see website).

Walk down to Craven Passage and turn left to pass underneath the station to Villiers Street. Turn left and then right into John Adam Street.

John Adam Street (originally Duke Street leading into John Street) is part of the development carried out in the 1760s by the Adam brothers. The north side of the street is largely intact from their time, although no.16, where the artist Rowlandson lived, has been rebuilt.

Walk along as far as the fine frontage of the Royal Society of Arts on the northern side (nos.2-8). It was at this end of the street that King Kamehameha II of Hawaii, and his wife, died of measles in 1824.

Retrace your steps and turn left into Robert Street, continuing into Lower Robert Street.

No.1 Robert Street was the earliest London house, other than the Inns of Court, to be built as chambers for individual gentlemen.

At the end of Lower Robert Street follow the bend around to the left into Adelphi Terrace.

You are standing on what was originally the Royal Terrace of the Adelphi development and from this viewpoint you would have been looking down onto the foreshore of the Thames, with vaults and warehouses under your feet. The building of the Victoria Embankment in the 1860s isolated the terrace from the river.

Walk along the terrace and then left into Adam Street. Walk up the street and pause at the junction with John Adam Street.

No.7 is an attractive Adam house and next to it was the home of Richard Arkwright (d.1792) the pioneer textile industrialist and the richest commoner in England at the time. It is a surprisingly modest home for such a wealthy man.

Continue up Adam Street to the Strand and turn right. Pause at the Savoy Buildings.

The Strand has been a major thoroughfare since the 11th century and has been constantly rebuilt, so virtually nothing remains that is not mid to late 19th century. It was a major shopping street during the Regency period and had a rather disreputable night life.

On the north side between Exeter Street and Burleigh Street was the Exeter Change (not to be confused with the New Exchange further along). Built in 1676 it was the location for small shops such as haberdashers, drapers and milliners, and for offices. Pidock's Museum, "a collection of diverse beasts and birds, only exceeded in rarity by those of the Royal Menagerie", was located, bizarrely, on the floor above. As the exhibits were all live and included a hippopotamus that Byron thought looked like Lord Liverpool, as well as lions, tigers and monkeys, the logistics of keeping them must have been incredible. In 1827 an elephant had to be shot by troops as it threatened to break out of its cage.

Opposite, in the basement of the Savoy Buildings, was the *Coal Hole* pub where the Wolf Club met. It was founded in 1826 by actor Edmund Kean who said it was for gentlemen whose wives would not allow them to sing in the bath.

A little further along on the same side, and also now covered by the Savoy Buildings, was the shop of Rudolph Ackermann – printer, publisher, coach designer and retailer-extraordinary. His Emporium at 101, Strand sold prints and artists materials and he was the publisher of the iconic *Repository of Arts, Literature, Fashions etc* (1809-29) that contains some of the most vivid images of Regency society. From 1813 he held a literary reception every Wednesday that was widely patronised by high society and literary and artistic stars alike. His was the first shop in London to be lit by gas. In 1827 he moved to 96, Strand.

Continue along Strand, turn right onto Waterloo Bridge and continue to the centre of the bridge.

The original bridge was built 1811-17 to the designs of John Rennie and opened on the second anniversary of the battle of Waterloo (18th June 1817) by the Prince Regent. After some subsidence in 1923 it was finally replaced in 1937-42. There are fine views up to Westminster and down to St Paul's.

Cross to the downstream side of the bridge and walk back towards Strand. Turn right down the River Terrace ramp to the river front of Somerset House.

There are loos behind the Civil Service Rifles war memorial and a café on the terrace.

Somerset House has seen numerous changes since it was first built in 1550. Enter from the terrace and cross the courtyard to the Strand entrance. The Royal Academy was here 1771-1836 and the Royal Society 1780-1857. Exhibitions and art shows were a fashionable entertainment during the Regency. The Royal Navy occupied one wing throughout the Napoleonic wars.

Turn right onto Strand and walk along to St Mary le Strand.

The first hackney carriage stand was established outside St Mary le Strand in 1631 and remained in operation until 1853.

Walk ends.

Walk 7: The British Museum to Covent Garden

Distance: 2.25 miles.

Transport: Nearest tube station – Tottenham Court Road. Buses 19, 38, 55, 73, 98, 390.

When to visit: The Sir John Soane Museum is normally open Wednesday to Sunday & Bank Holidays. The Hunterian Museum is closed Sundays and Mondays.

Useful websites:

British Museum: https://www.britishmuseum.org/

Sir John Soane's Museum: https://www.soane.org/

Hunterian Museum: https://hunterianmuseum.org/visit

Start at the corner of Oxford Street and Tottenham Court Road and walk up Tottenham Court Road on the right hand side. Turn right into Bedford Avenue (was Tavistock Street) and left into Adeline Place (was Caroline Street).

Just before you enter Bedford Square note the remains of the mews in Bedford Avenue to your right.

Bedford Square is a handsome, and intact, Georgian square with a wealth of period features. It was built 1775-80 and amongst its distinguished residents were Henry Cavendish the scientist who died there in 1810. Lord Eldon, the Chancellor, lived at no.6 (1802-19), and was visited here when unwell by the Prince Regent who refused to leave until Eldon appointed one of his cronies to Chancery.

Eldon's time in Bedford Square cannot have been comfortable. Besides being pestered by the Regent, he was besieged by Corn Law rioters for three weeks in 1815. With the mob on the doorstep and a noose dangling from a lamp post outside the house, he was only able to get to Parliament by going through the gardens of the British Museum, escorted by Townsend, the Bow Street Runner. Later, when his daughter eloped from the house with architect George S. Repton, the unfortunate Eldon was the butt of much satirical humour. (Ironic, as he eloped himself as a young man!)

Walk around the square clockwise and leave by turning down Bloomsbury Street (was Charlotte Street), then left into Great Russell Street to the British Museum.

The British Museum collection was moved to this site, then occupied by Montague House, in 1759. Stringent admission conditions were inflicted on anyone wishing to visit, including a written application for tickets. Only ten were issued for each of the three hours a day the Museum was open and visitors were closely supervised by the Librarian or Under-Librarian. Things became a little more relaxed in 1808 but general admission was not possible until 1879.

Treasures acquired (one way or another) during the late 18th and early 19th century included the collection of antique vases formed by Sir William Hamilton, husband of Nelson's lover Emma; the Egyptian antiquities, including the Rosetta Stone, that were captured from the French in 1801 after the battle of Alexandria and, in 1816, the marbles from the Parthenon, taken by Lord Elgin. By 1823 the house was packed and work began on the new building which can be seen today, with galleries being added well into the 20th century.

There is an enormous amount to be seen, but for Regency and Georgian exhibits go to rooms 46 and 47 on the Upper Floor. There are fantastic displays of fashionable jewellery from 1790-1850, porcelain, glass, *objets d'art* and even Napoleon's death mask.

Return to Great Russell Street and turn left.

John Nash's first houses can still be seen on the south side of the street – the one he occupied himself is on the corner of Bury Place (then Bury Street).

Turn left into Montague Street for a short distance to admire a well-preserved collection of 1820s houses.

Return to Great Russell Street, turn left and then right into Bloomsbury Square.

Bloomsbury Square dates from the 1660s when it was a highly fashionable address. The northern edge of the square was occupied by Bedford House which was attacked by rioting Spitalfields silk weavers protesting about a tax on silk in 1765. It was demolished in 1800 and replaced, as part of the Duke of Bedford's development of his estates, by the terraced houses which can still be seen. The gardens in the centre were laid out in the same year by Humphrey Repton and the statue of Charles James Fox was erected 1816.

There was more rioting in the square in 1780 when the Lord Chief Justice's house on the east side was sacked by Gordon rioters: two of the ringleaders were later hanged outside. The riots were anti-Catholic in nature and were prompted by attempts in the Papists Act (1778) to reduce discrimination.

The house in the south west corner with Bloomsbury Way (originally Hart Street) was the home (1816-29) of Isaac d'Israeli, author and father of writer and prime minister Benjamin Disraeli.

Cross Bloomsbury Way in the south-east corner of the square and cut through Sicilian Avenue to Southampton Row. Turn right into Southampton Row, cross High Holborn to the left hand (east) side of Kingsway.

Southampton Row and Kingsway were driven through the area in 1905, obliterating the old streets that were heavily congested by the increasing traffic.

Walk down Kingsway and turn left into Remnant Street – the "remnant" of this end of Great Queen Street – and on into Lincoln's Inn Fields. Continue straight ahead along the northern side to Sir John Soane's museum.

Lincoln's Inn Fields is the largest square in London and was kept as open ground after strenuous efforts by the members of Lincoln's Inn during the 17th century. Lincoln's Inn is one of London's historic Inns of Court for groups of lawyers that date back to the 13th century.

Prime Minister Spencer Perceval (assassinated 1812) lived at Lindsey House (1790-1807). There are handsome 18th century houses all around the square.

The main attraction, however, is Sir John Soane's Museum (nos.12,13,14). The museum is cramped and numbers are often restricted, so it is advisable to check for information on the website first. The architect Sir John Soane built the houses as his own home in stages between 1792-1824. He was an avid collector and the collections within the rooms, decorated in a perfectly-preserved Regency style, include paintings, casts, curiosities and antiquities. The result is a highly atmospheric and evocative Regency experience.

Leaving the museum, turn left and then right through a pedestrian gate into the square. Cross it to the far side and the Hunterian Museum, which is fascinating but perhaps not for the squeamish. If you don't want to visit, turn right from the Soane museum and then left down the west side of the square and turn right into Sardinia Street to Kingsway.

To quote the website, "The Hunterian Museum, named after the 18th century surgeon and anatomist John Hunter (1728-1793)... includes the display of over 2,000 anatomical preparations from Hunter's original collection, alongside instruments, equipment, models, paintings and archive material, which trace the history of surgery from ancient times to the latest robot-assisted operations. The Museum includes England's largest public display of human anatomy."

If you do visit the Hunterian, on leaving turn left and continue into Sardinia Street to Kingsway.

Cross Kingsway, turn left and then right into Kemble Street. Continue along Kemble Street which becomes Russell Street when you cross Drury Lane. Continue straight ahead.

Kemble Street and Russell Street are 19th century streets driven through a tangle of older thoroughfares. By the time you pass Crown Court the bulk of Drury Lane Theatre, now the Theatre Royal Drury Lane, is looming on your left. Theatres on the site date back to 1663 and Nell Gwynne made her debut here in 1665, David Garrick in 1742, Mrs Siddons in 1775 and John Kemble in 1783.

A new theatre was opened in 1794 and in 1800 an attempt was made there on the life of George III. The theatre burned down in 1809. The fire was watched calmly by Richard Brinsley Sheridan, the manager, as he sipped a glass of port "by my own fireside". Rebuilt in 1811-12, with a portico added in 1820, it is the oldest working theatre in London. Edmund Kean first appeared here in 1814 and Grimaldi, the clown, had his farewell benefit in 1818. There are sometimes excellent behind the scenes tours. (Ask at the box office).

Turn right into Bow Street.

Bow Street, famous for its magistrates' court and the legendary Bow Street Runners, preserves no trace of original buildings. The magistrates' court was on the western side of the street in 1740, with an entrance where the goods entrance to the Opera House now is, just north of the corner with Russell Street.

The second magistrate was Henry Fielding who, in 1749, founded the band of thief-takers who became known as the Bow Street Runners. They remained an independent force even after the Metropolitan Police Act of 1829 and were finally disbanded in 1839.

On the western side now is the Royal Opera House, more or less on the site of Covent Garden Theatre which dated back to 1732. It burned down in 1808, dispossessing the Beef-Steak Society who would meet every Saturday evening between November and June for a steak dinner. Members included the Prince Regent and his brothers the Dukes of York and Sussex.

The second theatre opened in 1809. It was so expensive to build that ticket prices were raised, sparking The Old Price Riots which went on for 61 days until the prices were reduced. Mrs Siddons made her farewell performance here in 1812 and the theatre saw the first productions in English of *Don Giovanni* (1817), *The Marriage of Figaro* (1819) and *The Barber of Seville* (1818). That building burned down in 1855 and the present one was opened in 1858.

Retrace your steps to Russell Street, turn right along to Covent Garden Market.

In the 18th and 19th centuries Covent Garden was a major centre for entertainment and a by-word for vice. As you turn left from Russell Street the building on the right-hand corner was the *Bedford Coffee House* where the Beef-Steak Society moved in 1809. On the left-hand corner was *Hummums Hotel*, a bagnio or bath house (a cover for a brothel) with the notorious 'Madam' Mrs Gould upstairs. Next to that was *Lovejoy's Bagnio* and the *Bedford Arms Tavern* and Bagnio.

Turn left, continue around the Piazza, turn left down Southampton Street and right into Maiden Lane.

Maiden Lane is incongruously named, given the location, and is probably a corruption of Midden Lane. It retains a few 18th century houses. On the right is *Rules*, the oldest restaurant in London, founded in 1798, although the splendid interior now reflects its Edwardian popularity. On the left is the back, and stage door, of the Adelphi Theatre. The present building dates to 1930, but the first on the site was the Sans Pareil (1806) which changed its name to the Adelphi in 1819. It was popular for burlesques, melodramas, farces and pantomimes. Further along on the left in Exchange Court is the site of the birthplace of the artist Turner.

At the end of Maiden Lane turn left into Bedford Street.

Bedford Street (originally Half Moon Street) was the location of the *Sign of the Green Canister* where Mrs Constantia Phillips sold condoms and other erotic aids from 1730 onwards.

Continue to The Strand.

Walk ends.

Walk 8: Trafalgar Square to Westminster

Distance: 2 miles.

Transport: Nearest tube station Charing Cross. Buses 15, 24, 26, 29, 87, 176, 91.

When to visit: The museums are open daily. Check Westminster Abbey website for special services: it is not generally open for visitors on Sundays and during services. This is a popular tourist area and gets very crowded during school holidays.

Useful websites:

St Martin in the Field: https://www.stmartin-in-the-fields.org/

National Portrait Gallery: https://www.npg.org.uk/

The National Gallery: https://www.nationalgallery.org.uk/

The Household Cavalry Museum: https://householdcavalry.co.uk/museum/

Westminster Abbey: https://www.westminster-abbey.org/

From Charing Cross station, turn left down Strand, cross the road and walk up the east side of Trafalgar Square to the steps of St Martin's church and pause under the portico.

St Martin's church is the only feature that a Regency Londoner would recognise of the scene today. In front of you, slightly to the right, and under the National Portrait Gallery, was the vast St Martin's Workhouse. The area occupied by the Square and the National Gallery was the King's and Queen's Mews and a chaotic jumble of other buildings.

If you want a coffee before starting the walk, the crypt of the church has been converted into a café and shop.

Cross the road to the National Portrait Gallery.

The National Portrait Gallery has a suite of rooms (17-20 on the second floor) covering the late 18th century and early 19th century where you can look into the faces of many of the leading lights of the late Georgian and Regency period, including Nelson and Queen Caroline, who we will be meeting again on this walk. There is an inter-active computer allowing you to search the collection by theme – you can find your favourite Regency character and buy a print of their portrait.

Leave the Gallery and walk back toward Trafalgar Square, turn right, climb the steps of the National Gallery and look out over the square.

Until its demolition in 1830 the King's Mews (architect William Kent, 1732) stood on the site of the Gallery and the area in front of you was a mix of buildings dating back to the Tudors, used at various times as royal stables, offices and a Civil War barracks. Shortly before the clearance there was even a menagerie. The Phoenix fire engine was stationed in the south-west corner ready to gallop off to deal with fires – so long as the property bore the Phoenix Insurance fire mark. But John Nash's Charing Cross Improvement Scheme provided for the whole area to be redeveloped and Trafalgar Square was completed by 1840.

The National Gallery was begun in 1833 to house the collection which had been started by the government in 1824. Some of the columns from the Prince Regent's demolished Carlton House were used in the portico.

Cross the Square to admire the bronze plaques around the bottom of Nelson's Column (erected 1839-42). They were cast from cannon captured by his ships and portray the battles of Cape St Vincent, Nile and Copenhagen and Nelson's death at Trafalgar.

Walk across Trafalgar Square from Nelson's Column to the bottom right hand corner, cross Cockspur Street and into Spring Gardens.

George Canning lived on the corner with Cockspur Street in 1799. Canning was Foreign Secretary 1807-09 and fought a duel with Lord Castlereagh over government policy. *The Picture of London* (1807) recommends Wigley's Royal Promenade rooms in Spring Gardens which were open 10am to 10pm, admission one shilling (about £3.50 now). The visitor could 'meet' two invisible girls who spoke or sang on demand.

Bear left along Spring Gardens to the Mall and turn right to Admiralty Arch (1908-11). Cross the road and go under Admiralty Arch on the left hand side.

From here you have a good view down the Mall to Buckingham Palace.

Go down the flight of steps immediately on your left, turn left and go under an arch and then left again into the remnants of Spring Gardens.

From here you have a good view of Nelson's Column and Trafalgar Square.

At the end turn right and then immediately right again into Whitehall.

Whitehall is a half-mile long street linking Charing Cross with the Palace of Westminster and has also come to stand as the shorthand for the seat of government.

Walk down the right-hand side of Whitehall past Trafalgar Theatre.

The next building you come to is 26, Whitehall, the old Admiralty building, set back behind Robert Adam's Screen (1760-1). This area held the houses and offices of the Lords of the Admiralty and what you can see today is very much what Nelson would have seen when he visited.

If you look up you will see radio masts on the rooftop. In the early 19th century a telegraph was in the same position sending messages via a chain of relays to Portsmouth and Deal – same idea, different technology. By tipping the porters Regency visitors could see inside the telegraph huts – apparently security was not taken very seriously, despite the country being at war with France.

Immediately after the Admiralty building, set back behind a wall, is Admiralty House, built as a residence for the First Sea Lord in 1786-8. It was to the Admiralty that Lieutenant John Richards Lapenotière, captain of the little schooner HMS *Pickle*, brought the news of the battle of Trafalgar (21 October 1805) and the death of Nelson. He sailed into Portsmouth harbour on 4 November and then took a post-chaise to London. It cost him £46 16s 1d and he drove non-stop except to change horses twenty one times. He was promoted to the rank of commander for his efforts. There are information plaques at the southern end of the Admiralty Screen.

Continue down Whitehall, passing the office of the Parliamentary Counsel, which was the Paymaster General's office in Nelson's time.

You next reach Horse Guards. Turn right into the courtyard between the two mounted sentries and stop to admire the fine range of buildings (1750-9) which were built to combine barracks with offices for the Secretary at War and related officials.

Walk through the central arched passageway into Horse Guards Parade.

This vast space was originally the tilt yard of the medieval Palace of Westminster and tournaments were held here. In 1852 it was the only space large enough to form up the funeral procession of the Duke of Wellington.

Turn left towards the walled garden of Number 10 Downing Street which forms part of the southern boundary.

Walk along to the squat black cannon which is a mortar seized by Wellington during the siege of Cadiz in 1812 and presented to the Prince Regent. The bizarrely magnificent carriage was made at Woolwich arsenal and must have been very much to the Regent's taste. Regency guidebooks refer to the mortar as The Prince Regent's Bomb. Cruel caricaturists changed that from 'Bomb' to 'Bum'.

Walk back to the right hand side of the archway to see a second gun, a 16th century cannon captured at the battle of Alexandria against the French in 1801. The gun carriage was made in 1803 and shows a rather strange crocodile and Britannia, who is gesturing towards the Pyramids.

Just to the side of the archway is the Household Cavalry Museum. As well as holding a fascinating collection, including Waterloo relics, it is possible to see into part of the cavalry stables and watch the horses and their riders behind the scenes.

Return to Whitehall, turn right and continue to Downing Street.

You cannot enter Downing Street, but you can look down it. A close of houses was built in c.1680, of which only numbers 10, 11 and 12 remain. Since 1732 Number Ten has been the official residence of the Prime Minister. Beau Brummell was born here in 1778 when his father was private secretary to the Prime Minister, Lord North. Number Eleven has been used by the Chancellor of the Exchequer since 1805.

At one time the Colonial Office was located on the south side of the street and it was here that Nelson and Wellington had their only meeting. What Nelson thought is not recorded, but Wellington was not impressed by the admiral's self-centred manner.

Continue down Whitehall which becomes Parliament Street.

During the early 19th century the road split into two – King Street on the west and Parliament Street on the east – and both ended in

Parliament Square. Now the block of houses between them has gone, opening out the vista to the Houses of Parliament and Westminster Abbey. The Regency Londoner would recognise the Abbey but only the great medieval Westminster Hall remains of the Palace of Westminster that burned down in 1834.

Cross Parliament Street at the traffic lights at the end and walk ahead along Bridge Street. Cross the Victoria Embankment onto Westminster Bridge. Stay on the downstream side and walk to the middle.

The Thames was not crossed here until 1746. The bridge was considered very handsome and was painted by Canaletto, but it was not all a scenic delight – Boswell indulged in sex in one of the stone alcoves and it was provided with pairs of basins at either end as urinals. The arches gave a good echo and people would play musical instruments to try it out as they sailed underneath.

In 1802 Wordsworth was inspired by the early morning view to write the sonnet *Upon Westminster Bridge*. The breeze had dispersed the heavy smog of coal smoke that usually obscured the view and he wrote, "Earth has not anything to show so fair..." The whole poem is on a small bronze plaque on the rail at about the centre.

The bridge was lit by gas in 1814. It suffered structurally when the new London Bridge improved the flow of the river and was eventually replaced with the present structure in 1862.

On the far side of the bridge, on the right hand side where you can see a patch of trees, was Astley's Amphitheatre, home to circus performances, equestrian exhibitions and various, very popular, extravaganzas. It was rebuilt in 1803, then twice again and was eventually demolished in 1893. Further along Bridge Road on the far side of the river were the new Bethlem Hospital and Coade's artificial stone manufactory.

Retrace your steps along Bridge Street, re-cross Parliament Street and walk straight ahead along the edge of Parliament Square, turning left at the statue of Canning and continuing past Abraham Lincoln. Cross at the traffic lights to the entrance to Westminster Abbey at the Great North Door.

For the Regency enthusiast the most vivid scene at Westminster Abbey must be the spectacular coronation of George IV in 1821 which cost £240,000 (over £22 million today) and from which his estranged queen, Caroline, was barred. She became frantic, running from door to door, but eventually retired, defeated and broken in spirit, to Hammersmith.

The Abbey holds hundreds of monuments and memorials and any visitor will want to browse extensively. However there are many of particular Regency interest and some of these are mentioned in the order of the route visitors take around the Abbey.

In the North Aisle close to the ticket desk are the statesmen and fellow duellists George Canning (d.1827) and Viscount Castlereagh (d.1822); Lord Palmerston (Secretary at War from 1809-22) and Robert Peel (Home Secretary responsible for the Metropolitan Police force in 1829).

Turn left into the congested Abbot Islip's Chapel to search for Sir John Franklin (who fought at Trafalgar and led Arctic expeditions in 1819 and 1823); Thomas Telford (engineer); Humphrey Davy (chemist) and John Philip Kemble (actor).

Continue round the ambulatory, into Henry VII's Chapel and round to the South Transept (Poet's Corner) where you will find plaques to Jane Austen, Robert Southey, Robert Burns, Keats, Shelley, Coleridge, Byron and Robert Adam amongst many others.

The route takes you into the Cloister and the Museum where you will find a stunning wax effigy of Nelson made in 1806 and dressed in his genuine clothes. There is even one of his hats with the green eye shade. It was considered a most lifelike representation at the time and gives a vivid impression of the man, including his slight stature.

You continue to the Nave with the memorial to Pitt the Younger over the Great West Door. In this area you will find Charles James Fox, shown with an enslaved man to commemorate his efforts to abolish the trade; Spencer Perceval, the Prime Minister assassinated in 1812; William Wilberforce, another passionate campaigner against the slave trade, and Sir Stamford Raffles, founder of Singapore.

Leave the Abbey by the Great West Door, cross the Sanctuary and go up Storey's Gate (left hand side of the conference centre). At the end turn left into Birdcage Walk, cross the road and enter St James's Park.

At night St James Park was a notorious haunt of prostitutes. Its regeneration began with the 1814 celebrations of the centenary of Hanoverian rule, the anniversary of the Battle of the Nile and the (temporary) peace following the exile of Napoleon to Elba. John Nash designed a seven-storey Chinese pagoda – which caught fire from fireworks during the gala display – and a bridge across the canal which remained until 1825.

The park was lit by gas in 1822 which curtailed the night time activities somewhat and the canal was remodelled to its present curves in 1827. There is a good view of Buckingham Palace from the modern bridge.

Walk ends.

Walk 9: The City From Bridewell to the Bank

Distance: 2.25 miles.

Transport: Nearest tube station Blackfriars. Bus 40, 63, 786, 788 to Blackfriars or 4, 15, 17, 76 to Ludgate Circus.

When to visit: The Bank of England Museum is not open at weekends, nor are most City pubs and shops. The Guildhall Art Gallery is closed Sunday mornings. Generally the area is more vibrant and alive Monday-Friday.

Useful websites:

St Paul's Cathedral: https://www.stpauls.co.uk/

Guildhall Art Gallery: https://www.cityoflondon.gov.uk/things-to-do

Bank of England Museum: https://www.bankofengland.co.uk/museum

Leave Blackfriars tube station into New Bridge Street and turn left down to the river and Blackfriars Bridge.

New Bridge Street was built over the lower course of the Fleet River in 1764.

The first bridge over the Thames here was fully opened in 1769. It rapidly deteriorated and was finally replaced in 1869 and widened in 1909. There are views from it of St Paul's and many of London's modern buildings. Immediately before the bridge the street widened into Chatham Place where the young Emma Lyon – later Emma Hamilton and Nelson's mistress – was employed as a servant by Dr Budd.

Walk back up New Bridge Street on the left hand side of the road to Tudor Street and turn left.

Tudor Street cut through the notorious Alsatia district, a haven for criminals where the authorities feared to tread. Ahead you can see the Inner Temple, one of the Inns of Court, home to communities of lawyers. On your right was the Bridewell. Built as a royal palace under Henry VIII, the famous Holbein portrait *The Ambassadors,* was painted there. It became a prison for vagrants, disorderly women and similar petty criminals and was finally closed in 1855.

Turn right into Bridewell Place, which demarcates the shape of the prison, and follow it round to the right, back into New Bridge Street. Continue up New Bridge Street, turn left into Bride Lane then bear left into the narrow St Bride's Passage. Continue ahead into Salisbury Square and from there right into Salisbury Court.

Salisbury Court was the birthplace of Samuel Pepys (out of our period, but I am very fond of him!) In 1814 thousands of copies of the scandalous memoirs of Mary Anne Clarke, the mistress of the Duke of York, were burned at her printers here after the duke agreed to pay her a pension and deal with her debts. The first edition of *The Sunday Times* was edited here in October 1822.

You can enter St Bride's Church from Salisbury Court. The story goes that the fine Wren spire inspired Mr Rich, a pastry cook of Fleet Street (d.1811), to create fabulous wedding cakes modelled on its tiers.

Continue along Salisbury Court to Fleet Street and turn right.

Fleet Street leads you downhill into the valley of the River Fleet. When you reach Ludgate Circus look left up Farringdon Street, formerly known as Fleet Market. The river was covered over to give space for the market between 1737 and 1829 and now, reduced to a mere drain, it still runs under the streets down to the Thames.

Cross Ludgate Circus to the left hand (northern) side of Ludgate Hill.

Ludgate Circus was built in 1864-75 on the site of the Fleet Bridge. Walk up Ludgate Hill which gives a fine view to St Paul's Cathedral.

Look up Limeburner Lane, the first street on the left. This follows the south-eastern boundary of the Fleet Prison and the curving modern bronze-faced building you can see on the left hand side follows the exact shape of the Fleet Prison's walls at this point. The prison dated back to the 12th century. The conditions were dreadful, even after it was rebuilt in the 1780s, and a succession of parliamentary committees called for reform to no avail. It was finally closed in 1842.

"Fleet marriages", by clergymen imprisoned there for debt, were performed until Hardwicke's Marriage Act in 1753 made them illegal.

Immediately after the entrance to Limeburner Lane was the site of the *Belle Sauvage* inn. It dated back to the 15th century and Pocahontas was housed here in 1616. It was one of the major coaching inns of London throughout the 18th and early 19th century with stabling for scores of horses. Coaches left for Farnham, Bath, Bristol, Cambridge, Cheltenham, Hastings, Leeds and many other destinations and it was one of the sights of the City for tourists. The inn was demolished in 1873.

Turn left into Old Bailey and walk along to the Central Criminal Courts.

The Central Criminal Courts were built in 1902 on the site of Newgate Prison. There was a gaol here from at least the 12th century. A new prison was built in 1770-8 but was severely damaged when 300 prisoners escaped during the anti-Catholic Gordon Riots. It was rebuilt in 1793 and a triangular area opened up in front of it that can still be seen today. This allowed for better accommodation for the public hangings that were transferred here from Tyburn in 1783. During executions the area was packed with spectators, many of whom paid premium prices for views from windows overlooking the area.

Henry Fielding called Newgate 'a prototype of hell' and the posies of flowers that the judges at the Central Criminal Courts still carry on formal occasions are a reminder of the appalling stench of the place.

Return down Old Bailey to Ludgate Hill, turn left and walk up to St Paul's Churchyard.

St Paul's Cathedral can be visited now or saved for a separate visit.

The cathedral is full of monuments with Georgian interest. Among the more significant in the main body of the building are: Wellington's vast free-standing monument; Sir John Moore (killed at Corunna, 1806) and numerous other soldiers killed in the Peninsula campaign; a statue of Nelson; the painter Turner; the admirals Collingwood and Howe and Sir Thomas Picton (killed at Waterloo). In the Crypt are the massive tombs of Wellington and Nelson. There are also monuments to Admiral Lord St Vincent and, next to the café, my favourite, Lieutenant-General Sir William Ponsonby, killed at Waterloo.

If you are not visiting as part of this walk there is free entrance to part of the crypt with loos and a café – from the west end outside, go to the left and take the steps down.

On leaving the cathedral follow the northern edge of the building along Paternoster Row, turn left into New Change and cross the road at the junction of Newgate Street and Cheapside into St Martin le Grand. Walk up the left hand side of St Martin le Grand which becomes Aldersgate.

This entire street was packed with old inns. Just past Angel Street, and almost opposite Gresham Street, was the entrance to the *Bull and Mouth*, another of the great coaching inns of the 18th and early 19th century. It was demolished when the General Post Office was opened on this site in 1829 (demolished 1912). Bull and Mouth Street formed the southern edge of the churchyard of St Botolph's, now Postman's Park, and a tranquil place for a rest or to eat a picnic. St Botolph's itself is now the London City Presbyterian church.

The area north of here was so badly damaged in the Blitz that there was widespread redevelopment, most notably the Barbican.

The Museum of London, which was in the Barbican, has now closed and, at the time of writing, work is in progress to relocate it to Smithfield.

Return to Aldersgate and turn left into Gresham Street. Continue along this street until you come to the Guildhall.

The Guildhall is the centre of civic government for the City of London.

Enter Guildhall Yard in front of St Lawrence Jewry church and cross the Yard to the Guildhall Art Gallery.

There are many interesting pictures, mostly relating to the City, and underneath are the spectacular remains of the Roman amphitheatre. The most dramatic Georgian picture (1798) is that of the actor John Phillip Kemble as Coriolanus by Sir Thomas Lawrence.

Return to Gresham Street, turn left, continue to Princes Street, turn right and walk down it with the Bank on your left to Threadneedle Street.

Threadneedle Street was named for the needles on the coat of arms of either the Needlemakers' Company or the Merchant Tailors. Opposite to your right is Mansion House, official residence of the Lord Mayor, completed in 1752. The bulk of the Bank of England is on your left. Built in 1788 by Sir John Soane, only the great outer wall remains: the interior of the Bank was rebuilt between 1925-39.

Turn left and walk along the front of the Bank and then left into Bartholomew Lane. The entrance to the Bank of England Museum is almost immediately on the left.

This fascinating museum walks you through the history of the Bank and there is plenty for the Georgian and Regency enthusiast to look at, from coins and banknotes to cartoons.

Walk ends but –

There are several old pubs in the area: here are three of them to finish your walk with some refreshment. (Note: these are not open Saturday or Sunday).

Turn right out of the museum, cross Threadneedle Street, turn left and then right through Royal Exchange Buildings to Cornhill. Cross Cornhill and turn left. Just past Birchin Lane turn right into the narrow entrance of Ball Court.

Simpson's Tavern in Ball Court occupies two former dwelling houses of the 17th century which were converted into a tavern and chop house in 1757. At the time of writing it has been closed, but a campaign is in progress to revive it.

If you continue through Ball Court past Simpson's you will arrive in Castle Court where you will find the *George & Vulture,* built in 1746, and reputed to have been a meeting place of the Hellfire Club. It is mentioned frequently in Dickens' *Pickwick Papers.* Return through Ball Court to Cornhill, turn right and right again into St Michael's Alley to find the *Jamaica Wine House.* This atmospheric Victorian pub is on the site of the first coffee house in London, the *Pasqual Rosee's Head,* founded in 1652.

Walk 10: Southwark & the South Bank

Distance: 2 miles.

Transport: Nearest tube station – Monument. Buses 15, 17, 48, 133, 344.

When to visit and useful websites:

Borough Market is open Thursday 11am - 5pm, Friday 12 noon - 6pm, Saturday 8am - 5pm. https://boroughmarket.org.uk/

The Old Operating Theatre Museum & Herb Garret is open Tuesday to Sunday (check Bank Holidays) https://oldoperatingtheatre.com/

Access warning: the Old Operating Theatre Museum & Herb Garret is only accessible via a very steep and tight spiral staircase.

Start at Monument tube station, turn left (east) along Eastcheap and first right into Fish Street Hill.

Fish Street Hill was the original street running down to London Bridge before the old bridge was demolished in 1831-3. Walk down past the Monument to Upper Thames Street. Opposite you is the church of St Magnus the Martyr: the large clock (1709) overhung London Bridge itself. Inside is a fascinating model of the old bridge.

Leave the church and turn left. Watch out for an opening onto steps up to London Bridge.

Old London Bridge was just downstream of the present bridge. Although it was shorn of its famous buildings (1757-62) and had been widened and refaced, the bridge during the first quarter of the 19th century was still the structure of nursery rhyme. It was very narrow – in 1722 three men were employed to enforce the first "keep left" rule in this country. Traffic jams were common and were the reason why there were so many coaching inns just to the south in Borough High Street. Passengers would disembark there to take more convenient methods of transport across the river.

The bridge was severely damaged in the winter of 1813-14 when the last frost fair was held on the frozen river and work on a new bridge was begun in 1824 and completed in 1831.

On the upstream side of the old bridge, at the point where the new bridge now runs, there was a waterworks with waterwheels that took 4 million gallons a day from the river to supply 10,000 customers. It was closed in 1822 as a hazard to navigation.

Cross London Bridge and admire the view. Ahead to the right is Southwark Cathedral, the church of St Saviour until 1905.

Once over the bridge continue down Borough High Street on the left hand side.

You are now in Southwark. This was originally not part of London, but a market town in its own right. It was also the destination for Londoners looking for a good time – brothels, bull and bear-baiting pits, theatres and ale houses all flourished from the Middle Ages onwards. By the beginning of the 19th century there were huge breweries, two hospitals and seven prisons, busy docks and numerous warehouses.

Go under the railway bridge and take the second on the left: St Thomas Street.

The area to the north of St Thomas Street was occupied by St Thomas's Hospital, dating back to 1106 and moved to make way for London Bridge Station in 1859. To the south is Guy's Hospital, founded in 1721. In 1993 the two hospitals were amalgamated in one Trust.

Renowned hospital staff in the 1820s included Richard Bright (1789-1858: pioneer in treating kidney disease), Thomas Addison (1797-1860: "father of endocrinology"), Thomas Hodgkin (1798-1866: prominent pathologist) and the surgeon Astley Cooper. Poet John Keats was a student who attended Cooper's lectures: he qualified as an apothecary but never practiced. On the right hand side of the street at no.8 is a blue plaque marking the site of Keat's lodgings in 1815-16.

Opposite is the Old Operating Theatre Museum and Herb Garrett in the roof of St Thomas's church. From 1703 the apothecary of the hospital used the roof space to dry and store herbs. It now contains a collection of fascinating, if gruesome, medical instruments and information about herbal remedies and medicines.

In 1822 an operating theatre for female patients was constructed in part of the roof space and this is still intact with its tiers where students would cram in to watch operations performed without anaesthesia. The patients would mainly be poor people – those who could afford it preferred to be operated on at home. The wooden operating table shows the marks of saws used in amputations and the whole room vividly conjures up the horrors of surgery at the beginning of the 19th century.

Turn left after leaving the museum and walk along to where the courtyard and old buildings of Guy's (1722) open out on the right.

The hospital must have been an imposing sight for its humble patients. Further to the south was Guy's "madhouse".

Retrace your steps back to Borough High Street and turn left.

Borough High Street was lined with coaching inns, each running back from a relatively narrow entrance. On the left-hand side of the street their ghosts remain – if you look at the pavement the curving kerb stone at the entrance to each little alleyway has the name of the old inn carved on it. Many of the inn names are preserved in the names of the alleys or in

Victorian pubs on the same site. The noise and bustle as the stage coaches arrived and left must have been incredible.

Pass King's Head Yard, White Hart Yard and turn left to find the only original inn left – *The George*. Only one side of its rectangular inn yard remains, but the building gives a fascinating glimpse of these multi-storied, galleried inns.

Continue down Borough High Street passing more old inn yards, At Newcomen Street turn left.

This is a Victorian street running over the line of King Street. Ahead was the large Black Horse Brewery. On the right is *The King's Arms*, a Victorian pub. Look up at the fine stone coat of arms on the front. This used to say GIIR, for George II, and was fixed on the Stonegate, the entrance to old London Bridge from the Southwark side, in 1728. When the gate was demolished in 1760 it was removed, the inscription changed to 1760 and GIIIR for the current king, and put up on a tavern that stood in Axe Yard.

Immediately to the south of here was the infamous Marshalsea prison where Charles Dickens's father was imprisoned for debt in 1824.

Retrace your steps to Borough High Street, turn right and go up to where the road splits. Walk up the left hand arm of the road with the statue on your right. Cross Southwark Street, turn right and then immediately left at the Southwark Tavern *into Stoney Street.*

Borough Market starts here and opens out to your right into a maze of spaces packed full of high quality stalls – a foodie heaven. The market dates back to the 13th century and during the 19th century was a fruit, vegetable, fish, grain and cattle market. There are numerous places to eat, and loos.

When you have explored the market return to Stoney Street and turn right. Continue to the end and Clink Street.

If you look right you can glimpse the replica of Sir Francis Drake's *Golden Hind* and also a great rose window, all that remains of the Bishop of Winchester's palace.

Turn left and walk along Clink Street.

This was the site of the Clink Prison, which gave rise to the expression "in the clink" for being in gaol. It burned down in 1780 during the anti-Catholic Gordon Riots.

Turn right when Clink Street ends (opposite the Premier Inn) into Bank Street and then left onto Bankside.

From Bankside there is a fine view of St Paul's and the north bank of the river. Behind you, *The Anchor* inn is a very old pub and, although the interior has been much restored, it does look the part.

There is a short row of 18th century houses immediately after the pub. Behind them was the vast Anchor Brewery, a testament to the huge demand for beer and ale in the early 19th century.

Walk along Bankside admiring the view. Go under Southwark Bridge.

The first bridge here was an iron structure designed by John Rennie and opened in 1819. It was replaced with the present, wider, bridge in 1921. Note the interesting engraved panels under the bridge depicting the Thames and its banks in Stuart times.

Continue along Bankside, passing the Globe Theatre, to the Millennium Bridge (2000) and cross the river. Walk up Peter's Hill to St Paul's.

Walk ends.

About the Author

Louise Allen is the author of more than a hundred historical novels set during the long Regency period and a number of non-fiction books about the era.

She has also written *Walking Jane Austen's London* (Shire Publications) which gives eight more walks for the Regency enthusiast.

Subscribe to Louise's newsletter and find all her books at:

https://www.louiseallenregency.com

Don't miss out!

Visit the website below and you can sign up to receive emails whenever Louise Allen publishes a new book. There's no charge and no obligation.

https://books2read.com/r/B-A-JZLND-GAXCG

BOOKS 2 READ

Connecting independent readers to independent writers.

www.ingramcontent.com/pod-product-compliance
Ingram Content Group UK Ltd.
Pitfield, Milton Keynes, MK11 3LW, UK
UKHW020825060925
7762UKWH00003B/340